★ IT'S MY STATE! ★

WYOMING

Rick Petreycik

Cavendish
Square
New York

Published in 2014 by Cavendish Square Publishing, LLC
303 Park Avenue South, Suite 1247, New York, NY 10010

Library of Congress Cataloging-in-Publication Data

Petreycik, Rick.
  Wyoming / Rick Petreycik. — [Second edition].
    pages cm. — (It's my state)
 Includes index.
  ISBN 978-1-62712-225-2 (hardcover) ISBN 978-1-62712-489-8 (paperback) ISBN 978-1-62712-236-8 (ebook)
 1. Wyoming—Juvenile literature. I. Title.

 F761.3.P48 2013
 978.7—dc23

                         2013036661

This edition developed for Cavendish Square Publishing by RJF Publishing LLC (www.RJFpublishing.com)
Series Designer, Second Edition: Tammy West/Westgraphix LLC
Editorial Director: Dean Miller
Editor: Sara Howell
Copy Editor: Cynthia Roby
Art Director: Jeffrey Talbot
Layout Design: Erica Clendening
Production Manager: Jennifer Ryder-Talbot

WYOMING

CONTENTS

State Flower: Indian Paintbrush

The Indian paintbrush was officially named Wyoming's flower on January 31, 1917. The Indian paintbrush has small, green-colored flowers surrounded by colorful leaves. These leaves can be red, orange, yellow, or white. The combination of the leaves and the greenish flowers makes it appear as if the plant has been dipped in a bucket of paint.

State Bird: Western Meadowlark

The western meadowlark is a songbird with an unmistakable flutelike chirp. The feathers on its wings and back are a mix of brown and white. The feathers along its chest are a bright yellow, with a distinctive V-shaped black mark beneath its throat. It became the state bird on February 5, 1927.

State Tree: Plains Cottonwood

Cottonwoods can be found along Wyoming's streams and rivers, especially in the eastern part of the state. Some cottonwoods grow to be more than 100 feet (30.5 m) high. Their thick, rough-textured leaves make a rattling sound when the wind stirs them as it blows across the plains. The plains cottonwood was first adopted as the state tree in 1947.

State Mammal: Bison

Bison, which are also known as buffalo, once roamed the Great Plains in large herds. Bison in the wild had nearly vanished by the start the twentieth century because of overhunting. However, thanks to programs and laws, today the number of bison has increased. A wild herd can be seen in Wyoming's Yellowstone National Park.

State Dinosaur: Triceratops

About 72 to 65 million years ago, this rhinoceros-like, plant-eating dinosaur was quite common in the region. The triceratops had three horns on its face—one short one above its mouth and two longer ones above its eyes. It also had a large, bony plate extending from the back of its skull. A triceratops's body was about 30 feet (9 m) long and 10 feet (3 m) high. These prehistoric reptiles weighed between 6 and 12 tons (5.4–10.8 t).

State Insect: Sheridan's Hairstreak

The Sheridan's Hairstreak is a type of butterfly. It received the title of Wyoming's official insect in 2009. These small butterflies often live in dry environments such as sagebrush scrub. The females lay their eggs in wild buckwheat leaves.

WYOMING

Yellowstone National Park · Powell · Sheridan · Devils Tower National Monument · Cody · Bighorn National Forest · Cloud Peak Wilderness Area · Gillette · Black Hills National Forest · Teton Range · Yellowstone Lake · Continental Divide · Medicine Lodge State Archaeological Park · Bighorn Range · Powder River · Belle Fourche River · Newcastle · Grand Teton National Park · Jackson Lake · Shoshone National Forest · Worland · Thermopolis · Thunder Basin National Grassland · Jackson · Bridger-Teton National Forest · Gannett Peak · Boysen Reservoir · Riverton · Casper · Douglas · Grave of Sacajawea · Lander · Medicine Bow National Forest · Glendo Reservoir · North Platte River · Torrington · Green River Rendezvous · Green River · Big Sandy Reservoir · Rocky · Pathfinder Reservoir · Laramie Range · Seminoe Reservoir · Wheatland · Fontenelle Reservoir · Big Sandy River · Mountains · Como Bluff Famous Dinosaur Graveyard · Kemmer · Rock Springs · Rawlins · North Platte River · Laramie · Cheyenne · Evanston · Green River · Flaming Gorge Reservoir

N
W   E
S

The Equality State

An old saying tells us that "variety is the spice of life." If variety makes things interesting, then Wyoming is definitely one of the most interesting states in the nation. The state's land area is about 97,093 square miles (251,570 sq km), which makes it the ninth-largest state in the country. Wyoming has breathtaking mountains, red deserts, towering waterfalls, dry plains, bubbling mineral springs, gushing water jets, and spectacular canyons.

Wyoming is situated in the western part of the United States, and its shape comes close to resembling a perfect rectangle. From east to west, the state measures 364 miles (586 km), and its distance from north to south is about 276 miles (444 km). Wyoming's unique geography consists of three major landforms—plains, mountains, and basins.

The Great Plains

Most of eastern Wyoming is a high, somewhat treeless area that is broken up by low foothills, mountains, and occasional buttes, which are flat-topped, tall hills. Eastern Wyoming is part of the Great Plains region. This region is a high plateau that

<table>
<tr><td rowspan="9">Quick Facts</td><td colspan="2">Wyoming's Borders</td></tr>
<tr><td>North</td><td>Montana</td></tr>
<tr><td>South</td><td>Utah</td></tr>
<tr><td></td><td>Colorado</td></tr>
<tr><td>East</td><td>Nebraska</td></tr>
<tr><td></td><td>South Dakota</td></tr>
<tr><td>West</td><td>Idaho</td></tr>
<tr><td></td><td>Utah</td></tr>
<tr><td></td><td>Montana</td></tr>
</table>

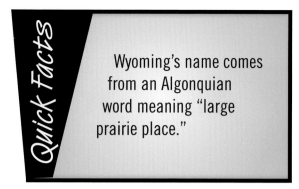
extends diagonally downward from northwestern Canada all the way to Texas. The area was once covered with tall grasses.

Today, the plains in Wyoming serve as excellent grazing land for cattle and sheep. Most of the area is too dry to grow a variety of crops. However, underground irrigation systems—which bring water to dry areas—have allowed farmers in some areas to produce corn, sugar beets, barley, hay, beans, and potatoes. Cheyenne, Wyoming's capital city, is located in this region. With a population of about 61,500, Cheyenne is Wyoming's largest city.

Wyoming's flat prairies are ideal for grazing cattle and other livestock.

Devils Tower was the center of action in the 1977 science fiction movie *Close Encounters of the Third Kind*.

The Mountains

Wyoming is home to a number of sweeping mountain ranges. In the northeastern corner of the state and extending into South Dakota are the Black Hills. These are a series of low mountains that average about 6,000 feet (1,829 m) in height. A well-known point of interest within the area surrounding the Black Hills is Devils Tower, a 1,267-foot-(386 m) butte that resembles a gigantic tree stump. Although the Black Hills are a relatively dry area, they are covered with ponderosa pines, which give the hills a darkish appearance when viewed from a distance.

To the south of Wyoming's high grassy plains are the Laramie Mountains. These mountains stretch across the state for about 140 miles (225 km). Near the northern section of the Laramie Mountains and almost in the center of Wyoming is Casper. This is the state's main oil-producing city. During the winter months, people who like to ski travel from all around the United States to Casper to enjoy the area's many fine, snow-powdered slopes. In the summer, Casper is also a popular destination for swimmers and boaters. Nearby Pathfinder, Alcova, and Seminoe reservoirs are perfect for enjoying water-sports activities.

To the west of Wyoming's Great Plains are a series of jagged mountain ranges that are part of the majestic Rocky Mountain chain. The Rockies extend from Canada all the way to Mexico. Wyoming's portion of the Rocky Mountains includes the Sierra Madre and Medicine Bow mountains in the south; the Bighorn, Wind River, and Absaroka ranges in the north; and the Gros Ventre, Salt River, Snake River, and Teton ranges in the west.

In the northwestern corner of the state is Yellowstone National Park. Established in 1872, it is the oldest national park in the United States. The park covers more than 2 million acres (809,300 ha) and features magnificent mountains, thundering waterfalls, and deep reddish-brown gorges. Yellowstone Lower Falls is located in the park. This is a magnificent waterfall that plunges 308 feet (94 m) into the scenic Grand Canyon of the Yellowstone.

Yellowstone also has about 3,000 hot springs and geysers. A geyser is a natural hot spring that shoots a column of water and steam into the air every now and then. The most well-known geyser in Yellowstone is Old Faithful. Like clockwork,

Mountain peaks are reflected on a lake in Yellowstone National Park.

almost every 74 minutes, it shoots a column of water into the air about 130 feet (40 m) high. The tallest geyser in the park is Steamboat Geyser, which sprays water as high as 400 feet (122 m) in the air. A variety of animals live in the park, including elk, mule deer, moose, bison, black bears, and a number of giant grizzly bears.

Near the eastern entrance to Yellowstone is the town of Cody, which was named after the famous frontiersman and entertainer William Frederick "Buffalo Bill" Cody. A popular town attraction is the Buffalo Bill Historical Center. Cody also has the Whitney Western Art Museum, the Plains Indian Museum, the Cody Firearms Museum, the Draper Natural History Museum, and the Harold McCracken Research Library.

Bison graze along a river in Yellowstone National Park.

A ridge of mountains runs back and forth from the northwestern corner of Wyoming all the way down to the state's south-central border. It is called the Continental Divide, and it plays a huge role in directing the flow of rivers along its path. The Continental Divide starts in Alaska, runs through Canada, the United States, and Mexico, and then runs into Central America. Rivers that start west of the Continental Divide flow toward the Pacific Ocean. Rivers that start east of the Divide flow toward the Atlantic Ocean and the Gulf of Mexico.

The varied and beautiful areas around Wyoming's mountains are popular attractions for hikers and campers.

Though it is completely surrounded by land, Wyoming actually contains 32 named islands. Many of the islands are located in Jackson Lake and Yellowstone Lake.

The Basins

Several basins dotted with sagebrush make up Wyoming's third major landform. Basins are deep, bowl-shaped depressions, or "holes" as Wyomingites like to call them. The basins' tops are surrounded by mountains. Some of Wyoming's largest basins include the Washakie, Green River, and Great Divide basins in the south. The Bighorn and Powder River are the large basins in the north. The Wind River Basin is located in central Wyoming.

West of Casper is the 320-acre-(130 ha) Midway Geyser Basin, which is often called Hell's Half Acre. Over a period spanning thousands of years, the constant interaction between wind and water has created an assortment of eerie-looking ridges, towers, and carved-out gullies. Many feel that these structures look as if they belong on another planet.

Climate

For the most part, Wyoming's climate tends to be cool, sunny, and dry. However, extreme weather conditions in both winter and summer months are not uncommon. For example, it is not unusual for winter temperatures to be a freezing -30°F (-34.4°C). On February 9, 1933, the temperature plummeted to a bone-chilling -66°F (-54.4°C) in the town of Riverside. That went into the record books as the state's all-time low. Wyoming's average January temperature is a shivering -19°F (-28.3°C).

Summer temperatures vary, depending upon the area of the state. For example, in the mountainous regions, summers are delightfully cool. On the other hand, temperatures on the low-lying eastern plains can be very hot. Residents of the town of Basin got a taste of just how hot it can get when the temperature soared to a record-breaking 115°F (46.1°C) on July 12, 1900.

Depending upon the region of the state, winter snowfalls can be light or heavy.

When it comes to precipitation—water that falls as either rain, sleet, or snow—Wyoming averages only about 13 inches (33 cm) a year, making it a rather dry state. Rainfall is very scarce in the plains and basin areas, but a common phenomenon in the higher-altitude regions. In the mountainous areas, snowfall is also a frequent occurrence, particularly in the Absarokas and Tetons. In fact, it is not uncommon for roads leading to and from both mountain ranges to be completely shut down between October and May. This is because of the ever-present threat of avalanches, which are great, overwhelming floods of snow that can occur when a snowbank suddenly breaks away from the side of a mountain.

The town of Dubois is home to the National Bighorn Sheep Center.

Wildlife

Forests cover about one-sixth of Wyoming's land area. Included within that area are three national forests—Shoshone, Bighorn, and Medicine Bow. The state's elevation plays a key role in determining where specific species of trees, plants, and flowers grow. For example, the colder, higher-altitude regions provide a good environment for the growth of mosses, lichens, and evergreens such as Douglas fir, Engelmann spruce, and lodgepole and ponderosa pine. Mountain mahoganies thrive in the lower-elevated valleys, as do wildflowers such as buttercups, goldenrods, evening stars, forget-me-nots, and arnicas. Cottonwoods, aspens, willows, and hawthorns, as well as sagebrush, greasewoods, yuccas, cacti, bluegrass, buffalo grass, and wheatgrass, grow in the dryer eastern plains.

Like its varied landforms, Wyoming also has a variety of animal life. In addition to swift pronghorns, there are moose, elk, bighorn sheep, and mule deer. Black bears, skunks, foxes, raccoons, and chipmunks can be found in the wooded areas. Near Wyoming's waterways you may find beavers, minks, and otters. Gophers, ground squirrels, cottontails, jackrabbits, coyotes, black-footed ferrets, prairie dogs, and snowshoe hares often make their homes on the plains.

Aspen trees, with their white trunks and yellow leaves, are a striking sight in Wyoming in the fall.

Many types of birds make their homes in Wyoming. These include magpies, juncos, chickadees, lark buntings, Bullock's orioles, long-tailed chats, western mockingbirds, and western meadowlarks. Wild turkeys, sage hens, and pheasants also nest on Wyoming land. Birds of prey, such bald eagles, golden eagles, hawks, and falcons, fly through the Wyoming skies. Waterbirds, such as swans, ducks, geese, pelicans, great blue herons, rails, snipes, gulls, and ospreys, are attracted to the state's wetland areas.

Among the many fish that inhabit Wyoming's rivers, lakes, and streams are bass, grayling, catfish, pike, muskies, walleyes, perch, and several kinds of trout. Many fishermen enjoy spending their days casting for these fish.

Over the years, the state of Wyoming has gone to great lengths to protect its wildlife. For example, in 1912, it set aside 24,700 acres (9,996 ha) of land near Jackson specifically for elk and other large animals. Known as the National Elk Refuge, it provides food and protection for about 7,000 elk during the winter months when natural sources of food are scarce. The added value of this large refuge is that it also keeps the elk from foraging, or looking for food, at neighboring farms. In addition to the National Elk Refuge, Wyoming has six other national wildlife preserves.

The state has also done a lot to protect plants and animals that are in danger of becoming extinct, or no longer existing. For example, an animal that has made a comeback in recent years is the timber wolf. For hundreds of years, the timber wolf roamed through the region. Starting in the few decades before Wyoming became a state, though, many settlers were determined to keep the timber wolf from attacking their livestock. For many years, the wolves were hunted and killed until they were nearly extinct—or gone completely. Beginning in 1995, however, a group of environmentalists reintroduced the timber wolf into Yellowstone National Park. Since then, the timber wolves' wild populations have been increasing. This is just one example of how Wyoming's residents treasure their land and all the life living upon it.

Wild mustangs run through parts of Wyoming's protected areas.

Herds of elk are protected at the National Elk Refuge.

Pronghorn

These graceful, hoofed animals roam the eastern plains of Wyoming in small herds. The pronghorn is North America's fastest animal and has been clocked at a speed of up to 70 miles an hour (112 km/h). When a pronghorn senses approaching danger and runs, its white rump flashes a warning signal to the rest of the herd, and the remaining pronghorns follow.

Grizzly Bear

The grizzly's long hairs on its back and shoulders often have white or silver tips, giving the animal a grizzled appearance. About 700 grizzly bears live in or around Yellowstone National Park and the bears are considered a threatened species, though their numbers have been increasing for many years.

Moose

The moose is the largest member of the deer family. Among its notable characteristics are a large snout, massive antlers, and a flap of skin—called a bell—hanging from its throat. Moose are very good swimmers, and in summer months, they can be seen along rivers and streams, feeding on water plants.

Mountain Lion

Also known as the cougar, the mountain lion is a member of the cat family. It has a small head and small, rounded, black-tipped ears. An adult male mountain lion measures about 8 feet (2.4 m) from its head to the tip of its tail. Although the animal is seldom seen, its lonesome-sounding cry can sometimes be heard during the evening, particularly in Wyoming's mountainous regions.

Ponderosa Pine

Named because of its ponderous (or bulky) size, the ponderosa pine averages between 100 and 160 feet (30–49 m) in height. This tree has a distinctive orange-brown bark and dark yellow-green needles. Some of these needles can grow up to 10 inches (25 cm) long. Most ponderosa pines live for about 125 years. Those that manage to escape natural occurences, such as rot, insect damage, or fires, can survive for nearly 200 years.

Forget-Me-Not

Found primarily in Wyoming's lower-elevated areas, this eye-catching wildflower has clusters of small blue flowers. According to an old legend, the flower received its unusual name because of a tragedy. A young woman's husband-to-be was picking these pretty flowers for her on a steep slope. While doing so, he fell and cried out "Forget me not!" as he died.

From the Beginning

Scientists and historians believe Wyoming's first residents were Paleo-Indians. These people likely entered the region around 18,000 BC by way of the Bering land bridge that connected Siberia (in Asia) to North America. Their descendants gradually moved toward the Rocky Mountain and the Great Plains areas. There, they gathered plants and hunted giant mammoths, bison, and other animals.

These Native Americans were quite skilled at making tools for hunting, too. Near Worland, Wyoming, scientists have discovered stone arrowheads and spear tips. These artifacts were near the bones of mammoths and bison that date back to about 9000 BC. They also found bone tools, as well as knives and axes carved from quartzite and chalcedony, two different kinds of stones.

Around 7000 BC, the region's climate began to change. Because there was not enough rainfall, the grasslands began to dry up, causing herds of wild animals that had been hunted for food—such as deer and bison—to move away. Because their livelihood depended on these animals, the region's Native Americans followed the animals. As a result, between 7000 BC and 5000 BC, there were hardly any human inhabitants in the area now called Wyoming. That began to change around 4500 BC, probably because of better climate conditions.

Throughout Wyoming's history, people have come to the rich land looking for a new life and new opportunities.

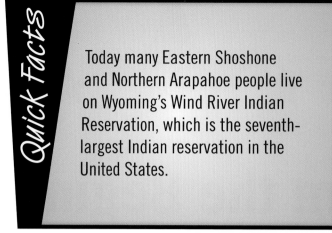

Over the next few thousand years, small bands of Crow and Shoshone Native Americans began to make their way into the region that would become Wyoming from the Bighorn, Powder, and Tongue River basins in the west. They were later followed by the Arapaho and Cheyenne, who came from the northeast from the areas that includes present-day North Dakota and Minnesota. Groups of Sioux from the areas of what would later become Wisconsin and Minnesota also made their way to the region.

While the Shoshone settled in the mountainous western region of Wyoming, the Arapaho, Cheyenne, and Sioux favored the grassy areas of the Great Plains in the east. There they made shelters out of branches and prairie grasses as well as conical-shaped dwellings made out of animal hides, called tepees. Other groups that eventually appeared in what would become Wyoming were the Nez Perce, the Gros Ventre, the Bannock, the Kiowa, and the Flatheads.

All of these Native American groups tended to be nomadic. That means they moved with the seasons, following animals they hunted, and never really settled down in a permanent spot. In addition to hunting deer and bison, they gathered wild fruits and vegetables and fished in the region's streams and rivers.

Horses would have a huge effect on the region's Native Americans. The horses were introduced in the early sixteenth century by Spanish explorers and missionaries who set up a mission in the region that would eventually become New Mexico. (Missionaries are people who move to new areas to spread their religion.) Many of the horses escaped from the Spanish and started living in the wild. The Native Americans spotted these beautiful, graceful creatures and

As more white settlers moved into the region, they often clashed with the Native American groups who lived there.

A traditional Shoshone hide painting shows a buffalo hunt on the plains.

decided that they wanted them. One reason for this was that the horses were fast runners. Soon, the horses allowed the Native Americans to easily move people and supplies. The horses also came in handy when Native Americans were hunting or warring with other groups. In fact, over the years, the Sioux and Cheyenne would gain great power in the region because of the large numbers of horses they possessed. Because of their use of horses, the Sioux and Cheyenne were able to force less powerful Native American groups to move away from the best hunting grounds.

New Arrivals

At the beginning of the 1700s, furs were extremely popular in Europe and in the growing settlements in North America. Fur was used to make clothing and accessories such as blankets. In 1742, Sieur de La Vérendrye, a French-Canadian military officer, fur trader, and explorer based in the French Canadian province of Manitoba, wanted to find a trading route to the Pacific Ocean. He sent his sons François and Louis-Joseph on an expedition that brought them into the region that is now northeastern Wyoming. In 1743, the two brothers saw the Bighorn Mountains but decided to turn back.

When they returned home to Manitoba, however, the brothers' stories about the region's fur-bearing animals—the beaver, fox, mink, and otter—stirred the curiosity of other French trappers and explorers. For the next sixty years, a few adventurous fortune-seekers from French Canada made their way into the land that now includes Wyoming. Many of them got along with the Native Americans in the region. They learned the native languages and customs, and some of these newcomers married Native American women.

Sacagawea, seen on the right, was married to a fur trapper named Toussaint Charbonneau. She was only about 17 years old during the journey to the Pacific Ocean.

In 1803, the United States, which had only been an independent country for a few short decades, doubled its size when it purchased the Louisiana Territory from France. The following year, President Thomas Jefferson decided to learn more about the new territory, with the hope of finding a water route to the Pacific Ocean. He commissioned Meriwether Lewis and William Clark to lead an expedition into the large unknown territory, which included most of present-day Wyoming. Although they never entered the area that would become Wyoming, Lewis and Clark did enlist the services of a Shoshone woman from the region named Sacagawea. She served as their guide and interpreter.

On the return trip, a man named John Colter was allowed to leave the expedition to go out on his own. He spent the next four years exploring the northern Rocky Mountains, including the Grand Tetons. In 1807, he discovered the Jackson Hole area and the Yellowstone region, where he was amazed by the magnificent waterfalls, jets of steam, and towering geysers. In 1814, William Clark published a map of the route Colter had taken.

The Fur Trade Grows

By the early 1800s, furs were very popular in New York, London, and Paris. They were quite fashionable, and consumers were willing to pay a lot of money for the latest cloaks and hats made from fur-bearing animals, particularly beavers.

Because furs were so popular, owners of fur-trading companies were faced with the challenge of making sure they got their furs to market as quickly as possible. One of those individuals was John Jacob Astor, a wealthy New

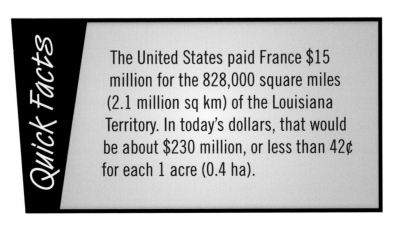

Quick Facts

The United States paid France $15 million for the 828,000 square miles (2.1 million sq km) of the Louisiana Territory. In today's dollars, that would be about $230 million, or less than 42¢ for each 1 acre (0.4 ha).

John Jacob Astor used the fortune he made in fur trading to buy large areas of land in New York City.

York businessman who owned the American Fur Company. In 1811, he asked Wilson Hunt Price, one of his agents operating in the region that now includes Wyoming, to take command of a trading post that was being built at the mouth of the Columbia River.

In 1812, Price sent Robert Stuart, one of his men, eastward to deliver some important messages to Astor. While on his journey, Stuart discovered a 20-mile- (32 km) wide opening through the Rocky Mountains. The passageway became known as South Pass, and it played a huge role in boosting the fur industry. It reduced the time it took to deliver animal pelts to markets, and also allowed trappers to hunt in newer, untapped areas.

The everyday lives of trappers and fur traders, also known as mountain men, were extremely dangerous and lonely. These men practiced their craft in unexplored territory and had to withstand bitter cold winters and dangerous animals such as mountain lions and grizzly bears. Because they worked in isolated areas, many of them would go for an entire year without seeing another human being.

A trader named William Henry Ashley helped change that sense of isolation in the summer of 1825. He set up a spot at Henry's Fork of the Green River where the mountain men could trade with one another and stock up on supplies. It became known as a rendezvous, and it evolved into a yearly summertime event that also attracted local Native Americans. For up to several months, the participants feasted, sang, danced, played cards, raced their horses, and traded their furs for gunpowder, knives, alcohol, tools, firearms, and other goods. In addition, many of them exchanged valuable information about newly discovered plants, animals, and trails.

In 1834, trappers William Sublette and Robert Campbell set up the Fort William trading post. This offered the mountain men opportunities to trade and to replenish their supplies more frequently than once a year at the Green River rendezvous. Located on the North Platte River in what is now southeastern Wyoming, this post became another chief meeting place for trappers and Native Americans.

So many wagons traveled across the land along the Oregon Trail that deep ruts have been permanently dug into the ground.

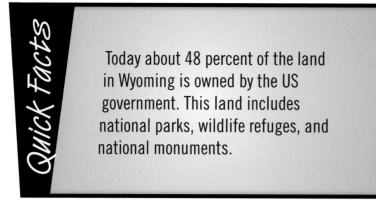

By the early 1840s, however, the fur trade had just about come to an end. Widespread trapping had nearly wiped out the region's beaver population. On top of that, consumers' tastes in fashion began to shift from beaver hats to hats made of silk. Understanding what this might mean to the fur trade, the famous fur trapper and explorer Jim Bridger retired in 1842 and built a cabin on the Blacks Fork River in what is now southwestern Wyoming. Within a year his home evolved into a trading post known as Fort Bridger.

Westward Movement

In the mid-1830s, many people in the United States began heading westward. They had heard tales of rolling hills, fertile fields, and pleasant weather along the Pacific Coast. For some people that meant opportunity as well as a welcome change. This was especially true for those who had experienced bitter cold Midwestern and eastern winters.

Missionaries were among the first to journey west. Marcus Whitman, a missionary from New York, had actually visited the region in 1835 and even participated in the Green River rendezvous that summer. The following year, two trappers from the region led Whitman and his wife, Narcissa, along with fellow missionary Henry H. Spaulding and his bride, Eliza, through the area. The two ladies were the first white women to set foot in the region.

By 1840, more and more people began moving west to the land that is now Oregon and California. Whether they were missionaries or adventure seekers, they all had to make the 250-mile-(402 km) trek across Wyoming as they followed the North Platte and Sweetwater rivers and then crossed the Rockies at South Pass.

When gold was discovered in California in 1849, the region attracted even more people. As news of the gold spread back East, tens of thousands of fortune seekers—known as forty-niners—gathered their belongings, made their way through South Pass, and then headed to California. Despite the number of people passing through, the land that is now Wyoming was not a place where people wanted to settle. They felt some parts of it were too bleak and treeless, while other regions were too mountainous. For most people heading west, the region was just a place where they could stop on their way toward greener pastures.

As more and more people headed west, they passed through Native American hunting grounds. Settlers killed many of the wild animals that the native people depended on for food. This angered the Native Americans. As a result, many natives began attacking the newcomers and their wagon trains.

US Army scout and explorer Lieutenant John Charles Fremont told the Congress that the settlers needed protection. So in 1846, Congress authorized the US Army to send troops to the region and build forts along the Oregon Trail.

Fort Laramie provided safety for settlers who were living in the new territory.

In Their Own Words

I have listened patiently to the promises of the Great Father, but his memory is short. I am now done with him. This is all I have to say.

—Lakota Sioux Chief Red Cloud

In 1849, military officials turned the trading post of Fort William—in present-day southeastern Wyoming—into an important military post. They renamed it Fort Laramie.

The forts that sprang up along the Oregon Trail beginning in the late 1840s provided protection for settlers heading west. The forts also served as centers of commercial activity. In fact, it was not uncommon to see all kinds of merchants in the fort selling flour, sugar, building materials, and other goods.

In 1851, in an attempt to put an end to Native American attacks on the settlers, Thomas Fitzpatrick, a friend of trapper and explorer Jim Bridger, and D.D. Mitchell, the superintendent of Indian Affairs, called for a council of Native Americans of the Great Plains region. About 10,000 Sioux, Cheyenne, Arapaho, Crow, and Shoshone met with Fitzpatrick, Mitchell, and US military commanders at the mouth of Horse Creek on the Platte River. There, representatives from all parties signed what came to be known as the Treaty of Fort Laramie. According to the terms of the treaty, the Native Americans agreed not to attack the new white settlers and to keep peace among themselves. The Native Americans also permitted forts and roads to be built on their lands. In return, the treaty commissioners agreed to pay the natives $50,000 a year for the next fifty years. This was supposed to pay for the damage the newcomers had done to the bison population and their grazing land.

However, Congress soon changed its mind about the $50,000 figure and reduced it to $10,000. Some native groups were never paid at all. This was just the beginning of many agreements with Native Americans that would be broken by the US government during the next thirty-five years.

In 1854, a white settler complained to Fort Laramie that a party of Sioux warriors had killed his stray cow. The army sent Lieutenant John Grattan and twenty-nine soldiers to a Sioux village near the fort to find the people who had supposedly committed the crime. They asked the Sioux leaders to hand over the guilty ones. When the Sioux refused, shots were exchanged between the soldiers and the Native Americans. In the confusion that followed, Chief Brave Bear was killed. The Sioux retaliated by killing Grattan and all of his men.

Treaties between the region's Native Americans and the US government were meant to keep the area peaceful and allow for American settlement. However, many treaties were not honored by the government, and peace was short-lived.

As relations between whites and Wyoming's Native Americans became worse, the American Civil War erupted in 1861. No Civil War battles were fought on Wyoming soil. However, the US Army had to pull troops from its forts in Wyoming to fight for the Union back East. This left many westward-bound travelers unprotected, and Native American attacks on the wagon trains increased.

In 1862, gold was discovered in Montana, causing another gold rush. John Bozeman, a fortune-seeker from Georgia, had cut a trail from Colorado to the Montana gold fields, and it ran right through Wyoming's Powder River Basin. This region was prime hunting grounds of the Sioux, Arapaho, and Cheyenne. All three groups, especially the Sioux, were angry. As their attacks became more frequent, in 1866, the US Army built Fort Reno and Fort Phil Kearny in northeastern Wyoming.

Between 1865 and 1867, some of the bloodiest battles between Native American warriors and US troops were fought on Wyoming's plains. However, by 1868, Chief Red Cloud of the Sioux had had enough and was willing to negotiate. A second treaty was signed at Fort Laramie. According to its terms, the Bozeman Trail, as well as Fort Reno, Fort Phil Kearny, and two other forts were closed. It was also agreed that no whites would be allowed to enter the land north of the North Platte River and east of the Bighorn Mountains. In addition, the Sioux and Cheyenne stated they would not stand in the way of a railroad that was being built across southern Wyoming.

Around the same time, a treaty was signed with the Shoshone at Fort Bridger. The Shoshone, under the leadership of Chief Washakie, were granted a 2.2 million-acre-(890,300 ha) reservation in the Wind River Valley. There was peace between the whites and Native Americans, but it was only temporary.

Gold and the Railroad

By about 1865, less than 1,000 whites were living in the Wyoming region, and most of them settled around Fort Laramie and Fort Bridger. That began to change. In 1867, gold was discovered at South Pass. Thousands of prospectors and fortune-seekers moved into the surrounding area, setting up several mining camps in the process. One of those camps became South Pass City, and within a short period of time, the town had close to 4,000 residents.

That same year, construction of the Union Pacific Railroad—a project that was designed to span the entire United States and its territories from east to west—reached southern Wyoming. Various coal mines along the railroad line were discovered and were mined to fuel the trains once construction was completed.

Six towns were established close to the mines, and one of them was Cheyenne. Named in honor of the Cheyenne Native Americans, the town was officially born on July 4, 1867. It became the Union Pacific's first terminal—or stop—in Wyoming. By the time the first Union Pacific train pulled into the terminal four months later, Cheyenne was a bustling city with close to 6,000 residents. Most of these people were men who worked on the railroad.

Other towns that sprang up along the railroad line were Laramie, Rawlins, Rock Springs, Green River, Evanston, Benton, Bryan, and Bear River City. By the time the railroad was completed, Wyoming's population had grown from 1,000 to 11,000 during a three-year period.

This hotel in Laramie was built near the newly laid railroad tracks.

On September 6, 1870, Louisa Ann Swain became the first woman in the United States to vote in a general election. Today a statue commemorating her vote stands in front of the Wyoming House for Historic Women, in Laramie.

The Wyoming Territory

As the population began to soar in the late 1860s, residents wanted to become part of a separate territory. At the time, the land that includes present-day Wyoming was part of the huge Dakota Territory, which also included present-day North and South Dakota. Decision-makers in Washington, D.C., listened, and on July 25, 1868, the Wyoming Organic Act was passed. The Wyoming Territory was cut from the western portion of the Dakota Territory. The following year, President Ulysses S. Grant appointed Brigadier General John A. Campbell as the territory's first governor. In addition, Cheyenne, Wyoming's first railroad town, was chosen as territorial capital.

Women in Wyoming were given the right to vote long before women in other US states.

Wyoming's first territorial legislature met on October 12, 1869. At this session, a lawmaker from South Pass City named William Bright proposed an idea that surprised many. Bright suggested that women be given the right to vote and to hold office on an equal basis with men. The Wyoming legislature saw the wisdom in embracing such a revolutionary, or new, concept, and on December 10, 1869, it became a law. This was the first law of its kind in the United States. When Wyoming later became a state, it was—and still is—known as The Equality State.

Wyoming's voters did not waste any time putting the new law into practice. On February 17, 1870, just two months after Bright's bill was passed, the voters of South Pass City elected Esther Hobart Morris to serve as justice of the peace. It marked the first time in the United States that a woman had been elected to such a position. Another example of women's equality in Wyoming was shown in Laramie in March 1870. For the first time, the town allowed women to perform jury duty in its district courts.

Ranching

In the 1870s, a number of cattle ranches began springing up in Wyoming. Grazing land in Wyoming was good—especially in the eastern section of the territory. From Wyoming's plains, the cattle were driven to railroad terminals like Cheyenne and then shipped to market. Throughout the 1870s, cattlemen built huge ranches in Wyoming. These ranchers became very wealthy and powerful. While most of them lived on their Wyoming land, some of them lived in other states and territories. Some of these ranchers even lived overseas in other countries. In 1879, a group of these cattle barons—another name for these cattle ranchers—formed the Wyoming Stock Growers Association. Because of the association's power and influence, its members were able to persuade the territorial legislature to pass laws that protected their land and business interests.

However, there were also many small ranchers in Wyoming, and they were denied membership to the Wyoming Stock Growers Association. In fact, many of the smaller ranchers found themselves disagreeing with the association's

Ranchers must protect their sheep from predators, such as coyotes, and bad weather conditions.

members. For example, the small ranchers tended to put up fences around their land to prevent neighboring cattle from entering their animals' grazing areas. The large ranchers, on the other hand, preferred the fenceless, open-range method of grazing. They also accused the small ranchers of stealing their cattle. As a result, there were often clashes between the two groups.

Sheep ranches were also popping up in the territory. Wyoming's large and small cattle ranchers often fought with the sheep ranchers. Cattle ranchers were unhappy that the sheep chewed the grass down to the ground, ruining the cattle's grazing land.

Beginning in the mid-1880s things started to go bad for ranchers. At that time, there were close to 1 million cattle grazing on Wyoming's rich prairie grasses. As a result, the prairies became severely overgrazed. A major drought hit the territory during the summer of 1886, drying up much of the land. A few months after that, a bitter-cold winter struck. The combination of both extreme weather conditions in less than a year took its toll on Wyoming's cattle, causing huge losses, particularly for the large, open-range ranchers.

To make matters worse, beef prices began to decline because there was too much beef on the market. Store owners were looking for ways to get rid of their extra meat, so they sold it cheaply. As a result, many ranch owners went out of business.

In 1892, some of Wyoming's cattle barons hired twenty professional Texas gunmen to round up small ranchers whom they thought were stealing cattle. They surrounded a cabin near the town of Buffalo, in Johnson County, and ended up killing two men in the cabin. Local citizens were mad when they found out what had happened. They went after the Texas gunmen, whom they called the Invaders. President Benjamin Harrison heard about this problem and sent in federal troops to solve the issue and to reestablish order. The event became known as the Johnson County War.

The events of the Johnson County War were turned into a television miniseries in 2002.

This dragline excavator loads a truck at a coal mine in Rock Springs.

Wyoming Becomes a State

Between 1880 and 1890, Wyoming's population more than tripled, growing from 20,789 to 62,555. Because it was growing so rapidly, many of Wyoming's residents and lawmakers felt the time was right for the territory to become a state. In 1888, the territorial legislature drew up and signed a petition, asking to be admitted into the Union. Its members then sent the petition to the US Congress in Washington, D.C.

The following year, fifty-five Wyoming delegates gathered in Cheyenne to create a state constitution. They discussed a variety of issues ranging from judges' salaries to the marking of county lines to women's voting rights. The US Congress ratified the constitution that the Wyoming delegates had drafted. On July 10, 1890, Wyoming became the forty-fourth state in the Union.

By the time Wyoming was admitted into the Union, other lines of work besides ranching began to become important in the state's growth. By the late 1880s, close to 2,000 laborers worked in the coal mines of Campbell, Uinta, Sweetwater, and other towns in southern Wyoming. The majority of Wyoming's miners were immigrants from Great Britain, Sweden, and China. They were seeking better jobs and better pay in the American West.

Oil also played an important role in Wyoming's growth. Although trappers in the early 1800s had spotted the black, tar-like natural resource and had learned how to use it for lamps, no one really knew how to mine it. That changed in 1883 when the territory's first oil well was put in place at Dallas Dome in Fremont County. Eleven years later, the city of Casper established an oil refinery, a place in which oil could be processed.

At first, Wyoming's oil was used mostly to fuel the Union Pacific Railroad's trains. However, with the invention of the automobile in the early 1900s, the state's oil had new uses. As a result, Wyoming's oil industry began to make a lot of money. A giant oil gusher in the Salt Creek Oil Field near Casper, in 1912, spurred even more growth. Many workers rushed to the state looking for jobs in Wyoming's numerous oil fields.

Improving the roads in Wyoming allowed more visitors to enjoy its beautiful scenery.

Farming had not really taken hold in Wyoming before statehood because most of the region was too dry to grow corn or vegetables. That began to change when the US Bureau of Reclamation was established in the early 1900s. The bureau authorized six dam and reservoir projects along the North Platte River. Once completed, the projects brought irrigation, or a way to water the fields, to Fremont County, as well as to Cody and Powell in the Bighorn Basin. Now with a plentiful supply of underground water, Wyoming's agricultural production began to steadily increase.

World War I and the Great Depression

In 1917, the United States entered World War I, and close to 12,000 Wyomingites—roughly 7 percent of the population—reported for active duty. Since oil was needed for the US Army's tanks and military vehicles overseas, Wyoming's oil was in very high demand during the war.

After the war ended the following year, the United States entered a period of prosperity. Some people had extra money to spend, and many of them began taking car trips, especially now that roads and highways had been created.

During the Great Depression, men who had jobs with the Works Progress Administration often lived in camps like this one near Wyoming's forests.

Grand Teton National Park covers about 310,000 acres (125,450 ha) and features opportunities for hiking, camping, boating, and many other activities.

Popular destination points were Wyoming's scenic Yellowstone National Park, which had become the world's first national park in 1872. Tourists also came to see the mysterious Devils Tower, which President Theodore Roosevelt had declared the nation's first national monument in 1906. Even more tourists flocked to the state when Congress created Grand Teton National Park.

Unfortunately the boom experienced during the 1920s eventually led to a bust in 1929 when the Great Depression hit. Like other Americans across the United States, Wyomingites faced hard times. Banks and stores across the country closed. Agricultural and fuel prices dropped a lot, causing many workers to lose their jobs. In addition, some of Wyoming's mines closed. Many people could not make a living. Families from the east traveled west looking for work. Many people were without money to pay for their homes or food. The federal government developed programs to help Americans during the Depression. These projects were set up to provide people with jobs while also improving the United States. These jobs included building roads, bridges, and other structures, and working in lumber camps.

In 1941 the United States entered World War II. The war helped Wyoming—and the rest of the country—recover from the effects of the Great Depression. The state's oil refineries resumed production to help power US trains, tanks, and airplanes both at home and in the war zones in Europe and the Pacific. The state's cattle industry also improved as large amounts of beef and beef products were needed to feed the military.

In addition, many factories around the United States were operating day and night to produce goods necessary for the war effort. That provided jobs for many Americans. It also meant that the factories needed more coal to help keep their machinery running. For that reason, Wyoming's coal mines were reopened. In fact, the state produced about 6 million tons (5.4 million t) of coal each year during the course of the war.

After the War and into the Future

After World War II, Wyoming's energy and mineral industries continued to grow. More oil was discovered in the Bighorn Basin and in northeastern Wyoming. In addition, trona—a mineral used in the making of glass, paper, soap, and baking soda—was found in the Green River Basin in 1947. Mining operations developed in that area. Soon the Green River region came to be known as the "Trona Capital of the World."

Another result of the war was the increased demand for very powerful weapons. The United States and other countries were working hard to create the most and best nuclear weapons, which are also known as atomic bombs and missiles. Uranium, a natural element that is found mostly in the ground, was needed to manufacture these very destructive weapons. In 1951, uranium was discovered in Wyoming's Powder River area. The US government was especially interested in this discovery. For a few years, Wyoming experienced a uranium boom that was very similar to the oil boom.

In the 1970s, Wyoming's oil industry received a boost when the United States was confronted with a serious oil shortage. The state's oil refineries were very productive. Wyoming's population continued to increase. This was, in part, due to the jobs created by the state's successful oil industry. Wyoming's population soared by 42 percent between 1970 and 1980.

Change was about to come to the state again. Worldwide oil prices began to drop in the mid-1980s. This forced Wyoming's oil companies to reduce oil production. In addition, many countries signed an agreement to limit the number of nuclear weapons in the world. This stopped Wyoming's uranium mining. As a result of these developments, thousands of Wyomingites lost their jobs. Almost 13,000 people left the state.

Cities, such as Casper, continued to grow as the state's economy improved.

Visitors to Wyoming continue to come to the state to see amazing natural attractions, such as Old Faithful.

In addition to these problems, Yellowstone National Park was struck by a series of destructive wildfires in the summer of 1988. Many tourists stopped coming to Wyoming, hurting the tourist industry. When the tourists stopped coming, many people who worked in the tourism industry—such as hotel and restaurant workers, tour guides, and museum workers—lost their jobs.

However, despite these misfortunes, Wyoming has an amazing ability to recover. Beginning in the 1990s and well into the twenty-first century, Wyoming's coal, oil, and natural gas production has been steadily increasing. A law was passed that requires out-of-state corporations to pay a special tax on minerals taken from Wyoming's mines. This money has helped the state's cities, schools, and highways. The fire-damaged areas of Yellowstone are slowly recovering, with new plants sprouting and thriving. The tourism industry has slowly improved as visitors come back to the state. In light of these positive developments, Wyoming's future indeed looks quite bright.

Important Dates

★ **Around 18,000 BC** The first Native Americans enter the region by way of a land bridge that connects Asia with North America.

★ **1743** François and Louis-Joseph de La Vérendrye, two fur traders and explorers from Manitoba, Canada, see the Bighorn Mountains.

★ **1807** John Colter, a former member of the Lewis and Clark Expedition, becomes the first white man to explore the regions that would become Yellowstone and Grand Teton Parks.

★ **1812** Robert Stuart, a trapper with John Jacob Astor's American Fur Company, discovers a pass through the Rocky Mountains. It becomes known as South Pass.

★ **1849** Fort William trading post becomes Fort Laramie, an important military post.

★ **1867** Gold is discovered at South Pass. The city of Cheyenne is born.

★ **1869** Wyoming women are given the right to vote and to hold office on an equal basis with men.

★ **1872** Yellowstone National Park, the first national park in the world, is established and opened to the public.

★ **1890** On July 10, Wyoming becomes the forty-fourth state in the Union.

★ **1893** Wyoming's first oil well is established at Dallas Dome in Fremont County.

★ **1906** President Theodore Roosevelt declares Devils Tower the first national monument.

★ **1951** Uranium is discovered in Wyoming's Powder River area.

★ **1988** Wildfires devastate Yellowstone National Park.

★ **2001** Governor Dave Freudenthal signs into law a bill creating a trust fund to preserve and to restore Wyoming's wildlife habitat.

★ **2013** Twenty counties are declared natural disaster areas after drought conditions make 2012 the driest period in 118 years.

3 The People

Wyoming and its residents are a mix of modern and traditional. The state was once a remote frontier outpost with little connection to the busy states and cities in the east. However, today, because of advances in technology, communications, and transportation, the Equality State is home to towns and cities filled with residents from all walks of life. The overwhelming majority of Wyomingites, though, still cling hard to the traditional values of the early settlers. That includes an intense respect for the land and trying to keep it as natural as possible. Whether they are city or country dwellers, Wyomingites have practically no tolerance for land development projects that threaten forests, mountains, plains, or the animals that live there.

Despite its large land area, Wyoming has the smallest total population in the country. Some cities in the United States, such as Seattle, Washington, have more residents than the entire state of Wyoming. Wyoming's cities are not heavily populated when compared to other states, and many communities and towns are spread out. As a result, Wyoming ranks forty-ninth among the fifty states when it comes to population density. Population density refers to the number of people living within an area, such as the number of people living in each 1 square mile (2.6 sq km) of land. On average, fewer than six people live on each 1 square mile (2.6 sq km) of Wyoming land.

Many Wyomingites are the descendants of the settlers who came to the region more than one hundred years ago.

Wyoming's low population density means there is a lot of space for residents to enjoy the great outdoors.

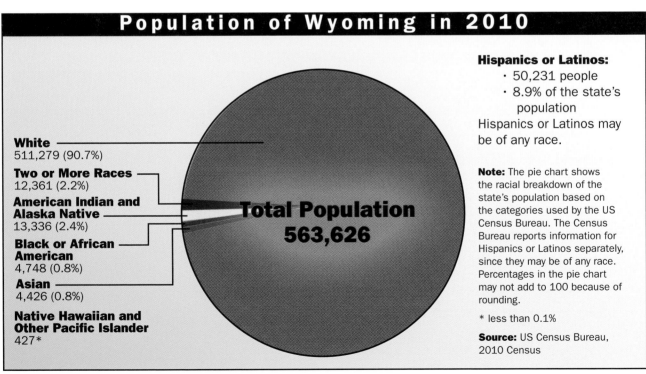

Population of Wyoming in 2010

White
511,279 (90.7%)

Two or More Races
12,361 (2.2%)

American Indian and Alaska Native
13,336 (2.4%)

Black or African American
4,748 (0.8%)

Asian
4,426 (0.8%)

Native Hawaiian and Other Pacific Islander
427*

Total Population 563,626

Hispanics or Latinos:
- 50,231 people
- 8.9% of the state's population

Hispanics or Latinos may be of any race.

Note: The pie chart shows the racial breakdown of the state's population based on the categories used by the US Census Bureau. The Census Bureau reports information for Hispanics or Latinos separately, since they may be of any race. Percentages in the pie chart may not add to 100 because of rounding.

* less than 0.1%

Source: US Census Bureau, 2010 Census

The town of Jackson manages to prosper because of a thriving tourism industry.

Wyoming's population is spread out, but that does not mean that everybody lives on a ranch, or farm, or any other large piece of land out in the countryside. In fact, over half of all Wyomingites are classified as urban dwellers. The US Census Bureau—the government agency that collects information about the country's population and economy—defines urban dwellers as people who live in towns or cities of 2,500 people or more. The majority of Wyomingites live in the southern portion of the state along Interstate 80 and the Union Pacific railroad line.

In Wyoming—as in all states—more people live in the cities or towns with more job opportunities. With a population of about 61,500, Cheyenne, the state's capital, is the largest city in Wyoming. It is also a major commercial, industrial, and transportation center. The next largest city, with around 57,800 people, is Casper. This city is Wyoming's oil capital and chief manufacturing center. Laramie, the state's third-largest city and the home of the University of Wyoming and several museums, has just a little more than 31,600 residents.

Though their populations are smaller, other cities are important centers for Wyoming's mining and agricultural businesses. Rock Springs, Gillette, and Sheridan each have populations between 17,000 and 31,000 residents. Wyoming also has many small towns. It is not unusual for some of these towns to have populations of fewer than 50 people!

Famous Wyomingites

Esther Hobart Morris: Judge

In 1870, the people of South Pass City in the Wyoming Territory elected Esther Hobart Morris as justice of the peace. She was the first woman in the modern world elected to such a position, and in an eight-month span she tried fifty cases. Susan B. Anthony, the famous suffragist leader who fought for women's rights, called Morris the "Mother of Women's Suffrage" because she thought Morris was helping in the fight for women to have more political power.

Matthew Fox: Actor

Matthew Fox was born in Pennsylvania, but moved with his parents to the Wind River Indian Reservation when he was just a year old. Fox has starred on hit television series such as *Party of Five* and *Lost*, and he appeared in the 2013 film *World War Z*.

Buffalo Bill Cody: Frontiersman and Entertainer

At the age of fourteen, William Frederick "Buffalo Bill" Cody, was a rider for the Pony Express. He later made headlines for his hunting ability, with some reports saying he killed 4,280 bison. In the 1890s, Buffalo Bill became famous around the world when he put together the first traveling Wild West show. This was an extravaganza featuring staged gunfights, stampedes, and battles between cowboys and Native Americans. Buffalo Bill died in 1917, but a museum and celebrations in Wyoming honor his memory.

Washakie: Native American Leader

Washakie was a Shoshone warrior who was chief of the Eastern Band of the Shoshone living in Wyoming. Though he was fierce in battle, Washakie also fought for peace between Native Americans and the white settlers. Washakie and some of his people often helped settlers travel through the untamed lands. In 1868, he negotiated a treaty with the US government that allowed the building of railroads through Shoshone lands and maintained peace between the settlers and the Native Americans. Washakie died in 1900 on the Shoshone Reservation.

Nellie Tayloe Ross: Public Official

Trained as a kindergarten teacher, Nellie Tayloe Ross was elected governor of Wyoming in 1924. She was the first female in the United States to hold the position of governor. After finishing her term as governor, she became director of the US Mint, a government agency in charge of duties such as producing and distributing coins. Ross died in 1977.

Chris LeDoux: Rodeo Champion and Musician

Chris LeDoux grew up in Texas and Wyoming and dreamed of competing in rodeos. In the 1960s and 1970s, LeDoux competed in the rodeo circuit, becoming a well-known and respected bareback rider. However, LeDoux always loved writing and playing music and pursued that dream instead. He became famous for his country songs about life in the rodeo, cowboys, and the West. LeDoux kept his ties to the land and lived on a ranch in Kaycee, Wyoming. LeDoux died of cancer in 2005 at the age of fifty-six.

Wyomingites

More than 93 percent of Wyomingites are white. Many of them are the descendants of the state's early English, German, and Irish settlers who came to the territory in the late nineteenth century. Most of these settlers started out as cattle ranchers, sheepherders, or farmers.

Throughout Wyoming's history, other immigrant groups have made their way into the state. These include the Italians and Greeks, who worked in the state's gold and coal mines, and Russians, who prospered growing sugar beets. Chinese immigrants also came to Wyoming to work on the railroads or in the mines.

Today, African Americans make up about 1.5 percent of the population. Asians make up about 0.9 percent. A little more than 9 percent of the state's residents are of Hispanic or Latino heritage. Some of Wyoming's Hispanic residents are descendants of Basque sheepherders who came to the state toward the end of the nineteenth century. The Basques are from the Pyrenees Mountain region of Spain, where they are well known for their skills at herding sheep and goats. Many Basques moved to Wyoming because they saw similarities between the state's plains and those of their homeland in Spain.

These Arapaho youth practice using their bows and arrows on the Wind River Indian Reservation.

Native Americans

Before any white explorers or settlers arrived, Native Americans were the only ones living in the region. Today, however, they make up only about 2.6 percent of the state's total population. The largest Native American groups within the state are the Arapaho and the Shoshone.

There are Native Americans living in the towns and cities of Wyoming. However, nearly all of the Northern Arapaho and Eastern Shoshone live on more than 2 million acres (809,300 ha) of reservation land called the Wind River Indian Reservation. The Arapaho live in the southern section of the reservation. They have settlements at Ethete, Arapaho, and St. Stephens. The Shoshone make their homes on the reservation's northern, western, and south-central portions. The Shoshone's major settlements are at Fort Washakie, Crowheart, and Wind River.

Both native groups own most of the reservation land, some of which contains coal, oil, and natural gas. If the tribes allow a petroleum, natural gas, or mining company to use the resources from the area, that company must pay the Native Americans a royalty. This means that the Native Americans receive a share of the money that is made when coal, oil, and natural gas is taken from their land and sold.

Four generations of Arapaho women who have lived on the Wind River Indian Reservation pose for this picture.

MAKING A DREAM CATCHER

The Native Americans of the Great Plains believed that both good and bad dreams were in the air. A dream catcher was used so that good dreams would pass through the open spaces and visit the sleeping person. Bad dreams would remain caught in the web until the morning Sun melted them away. Dream catchers were hung in tepees or attached to a baby's cradleboard. You can use your dream catcher as a colorful wall decoration.

WHAT YOU NEED:

Plastic lid from a coffee can

Scissors

Double-sided tape

Hole puncher

Yarn in 3 or 4 different colors

10–12 small beads (with holes

    wide enough to fit yarn)

3 feathers (available at craft stores)

   Ask an adult to help you cut the center out of the plastic lid. The rim that is left should be about 1 inch (2.5 cm) wide.

   Cut short strips of double-sided tape and spread these around the rim. The tape will hold the yarn in place when you start wrapping the yarn.

Wind the yarn tightly around the rim. About one-third of the way around, cut the yarn and tie it to the rim. Switch to another color and continue, changing color one more time.

When the rim is completely covered, separate two strands of yarn and use the hole puncher to make a hole near the inner edge of the rim. Repeat this in different parts of the rim until you have eight holes.

Cut a 24-inch-(61 cm) long piece of yarn. Tie one end through one of the holes, then weave it through another hole in the rim. Repeat this process in a random pattern to make a weblike design. Add a bead to the yarn every now and then to add color to the web.

When you finish making the web, push the yarn back in place to cover the holes on the rim.

Tie a short piece of yarn into a loop around the rim for hanging your dream catcher.

Tie three short pieces of yarn to the bottom rim. String three beads on each piece of yarn and tie a feather on each piece of yarn.

Hang your dream catcher and have pleasant dreams!

Calendar of Events

★ Ice-Fishing Derby

Held at Saratoga Lake each January, this fun event challenges participants to brave the freezing cold and compete for cash prizes. There are even prizes awarded for the best hut, or fishing shelter, and best fish story.

★ Cinco De Mayo Fiesta

This fun-filled event, held on the first Saturday in May in Evanston, kicks off in the morning with a community pride parade. Afternoon events include a tortilla-eating contest, a Mexican yell, or grita, contest, a piñata-breaking contest, a children's fair, and a salsa-tasting contest. In addition, mariachi bands and traditional dancers provide nonstop entertainment. Festivities come to a dramatic close in the evening with a spectacular fireworks display and a community dance.

★ Cheyenne Celtic Musical Arts Festival

This event, held in June at the Cheyenne Depot Museum, celebrates the Irish heritage of many Wyoming residents. There is a parade, live music, pipe bands, and Irish step dancing, as well as a fiddle contest and the "Calling of the Clans."

★ Indian Sun Dances

Each July, Wyoming's Eastern Shoshone and Northern Arapaho participate in various Sun dances, which are ancient spiritual rituals that have been passed on from generation to generation. The Sun dances are held on the Wind River Indian Reservation.

★ Buffalo Bill Cody Stampede Rodeo

Many believe that this four-day rodeo is the country's best large outdoor rodeo. It is held in Cody and does an excellent job of recreating the level of excitement and drama that marked Buffalo Bill's original Wild West shows. In addition to plenty of riding and roping activities, there are rodeo entertainers, parades, clowns, and more.

★ Gold Rush Days

Each July, South Pass City celebrates Wyoming's colorful mining history with Gold Rush Days. Held at South Pass City State Historic Site, the events include a traditional baseball game and a mining contest in which contestants drill holes into solid rock with traditional mining tools. Children also get the chance to pan for gold in the cool waters of Willow Creek.

★ Wyoming State Fair

An event that seems to get bigger and bigger every year is the Wyoming State Fair, which is held every August in Douglas. In addition to livestock shows, there are creative exhibits that include a best hobby collection, 4-H technology division display, and projects done by local Boy Scouts and Girl Scouts. On the more humorous side, there's also a rubber chicken relay race!

★ Jackson Hole Fall Arts Festival

Jackson Hole is well known for its flourishing artist community. The area has been hosting an art fair since the late 1980s, and it is one of the best and most well attended in the United States. The festival showcases visual arts, such as sculpture, pottery, and painting; performing arts, such as music; and culinary arts, such as cooking and baking. The festival also celebrates folk art and traditional Native American arts and crafts.

How the Government Works

Public officials in Wyoming define a city as a community with a population of at least 4,000. A town has between 150 and 4,000 residents. Wyoming has more than 100 cities and towns. Most of the state's cites are governed by a mayor and a city council. The cities and towns are grouped together—according to where they are located—to form counties. A county board of commissioners governs each one of Wyoming's twenty-three counties. There are three to five commissioners on each board, and they are elected to four-year terms. In addition to the county commissioners, other elected Wyoming county officials include county clerks, treasurers, and sheriffs.

On a statewide level, a governor who is elected to a four-year term heads Wyoming. The state also has representatives at the national level. Voters elect two members for the US Senate in Washington, D.C., and one member of the US House of Representatives.

How a New Law Is Created

When a law is proposed, it is first called a bill. As in other states, bills in Wyoming are often written and proposed in response to the concerns of ordinary, everyday citizens. After a bill is first introduced, it is given to a standing committee of the state senate or house of representatives. There it is considered and discussed by

State legislators meet at the Capitol in Cheyenne.

the members of the committee. The committee then votes on the bill to give it a "pass" or "do not pass" recommendation. If the committee passes the bill, it will be discussed and debated by members of that house. After the bill is discussed, debated, and possibly changed, the members of that chamber take a vote. If enough members vote for the bill, it goes to the other chamber. The second house discusses, debates, and votes on the bill. If it passes in the second house without any amendments, or changes, being attached to it, it is immediately sent to the governor to sign into law. If the second house amends the bill, however, it is sent back to the first house to determine whether the members of the first house agree with the amendments. If they do not agree, the bill is given to a conference committee to iron out the differences and to reach a compromise. The conference committee then writes a report on the bill, which is again voted on by both houses.

If both houses pass the bill, it is sent to the governor for his or her final review. If the governor signs the bill, it becomes law. If the governor vetoes, or rejects, the bill, however, it can still be passed. The two houses can vote again, and if there are enough votes in both houses, the bill will be passed.

If there is something you feel strongly about in your community or your state, you can try contacting your local legislators. You can make a difference!

Branches of Government

EXECUTIVE ★ ★ ★ ★ ★ ★ ★ ★

Wyoming's executive branch is charged with making sure that the state's laws are carried out. A governor, who is elected to a four-year term, heads the branch. Other members of the executive branch are the secretary of state, auditor, treasurer, and superintendent of public instruction. Like the governor, each of these people is elected to a four-year term.

LEGISLATIVE ★ ★ ★ ★ ★ ★ ★ ★

Wyoming's legislative branch is in charge of making or changing the state's laws. It is divided into two houses, called the senate and the house of representatives. The senate has thirty members, called senators, who are elected to four-year terms. The house of representatives has sixty members who are elected to two-year terms.

JUDICIAL ★ ★ ★ ★ ★ ★ ★ ★

The judicial branch of Wyoming's state government is a court system that is responsible for interpreting the laws that the state's legislature passes. Wyoming's highest court is the supreme court, which has five justices who serve eight-year terms. The state also has nine district courts, police courts, municipal courts, and justice of the peace courts.

Making a Living

The industries that have helped Wyoming's economy grow and prosper have changed throughout the state's colorful history. Mining and cattle ranching were the most important industries in the late nineteenth century. Then farming took the lead during the beginning of the twentieth century. Petroleum (oil) and natural gas extraction were popular in the 1970s and 1980s. As the twenty-first century began, mining once again became one of the most important parts of Wyoming's economy. The service industry—which includes any jobs that provide a service to people—is also a key part of the state's success.

Mining

Mining is huge in Wyoming, making up about one-third of its gross state product, or GSP. The gross state product is the value of all goods and services provided by a state during a specific time period. The state ranks high in coal production, gas production, and petroleum extraction.

The state's most important mineral is natural gas, and in 2002, Wyoming produced 2.2 trillion cubic feet (62.2 billion cubic m) of it. Most of Wyoming's natural gas production takes place in Sweetwater, Campbell, Sublette, and Fremont counties.

Coal is Wyoming's second most important mineral. Wyomingites are proud of the fact that most of the state's coal is low in sulfur, a type of natural element.

For centuries, Wyomingites have made a living off of the land.

Wyoming's Industries and Workers (June 2013)

Industry	Number of People Working in That Industry	Percentage of Labor Force Working in That Industry
Farming	3,200	1.1%
Mining and Logging	25,400	8.6%
Construction	23,600	8%
Manufacturing	9,500	3.2%
Trade, Transportation, and Utilities	55,200	18.7%
Information	3,800	1.3%
Financial Activities	10,800	3.6%
Professional & Business Services	17,200	5.8%
Education & Health Services	26,900	9.1%
Leisure & Hospitality	34,500	11.7%
Other Services	10,500	3.5%
Government	73,600	25%
Totals	**294,200**	**99.6%**

Notes: Figures above do not include people in the armed forces.
"Professionals" includes people such as doctors and lawyers.

Source: U.S. Bureau of Labor Statistics

This helps cut down on pollution when it is burned as a fuel, making their coal very desirable. In 2011, Wyoming's coal mines, the majority of which are located in Campbell and Carbon counties, produced more than 438 million tons (397 million t) of coal. It is no wonder that Wyoming is the leading coal producer in the United States.

Petroleum also plays an important part in Wyoming's economy. Almost all of Wyoming's twenty-three counties produce oil, but the counties that produce the most are Park, Natrona, Campbell, Fremont, Hot Springs, and Sweetwater.

Wyoming leads the United States in the production of trona—a grayish-yellowish mineral consisting of sodium, carbon, and water. Found deep below Earth's surface near Green River, the mineral is primarily made into sodium carbonate. This is then used to manufacture glass, pulp and paper, detergents, and chemicals.

Other important minerals that are native to Wyoming are agate, jade, diamonds, limestone, marble, gold, sapphires, rubies, copper, gypsum, and bentonite, a type of clay used in drilling oil wells.

Uranium, a radioactive element used in the production of nuclear energy and weapons, is also found in Wyoming. During the 1970s, the state had a booming uranium business. However that came to a halt in the early 1980s because of foreign competition, and because many countries agreed to limit the production of nuclear weapons.

Agriculture

Since the early twentieth century, agriculture's importance to Wyoming's economy has decreased. In fact, of the state's 294,200 workers, only about 3,200 are involved in farming or agricultural services. However, Wyoming still plays an important role in supplying a large amount of food to businesses and residents within the state as well as to people living in other states. Wyoming has about 11,000 farms and ranches that each have an average size of 2,726 acres (1,103 ha). The state uses about 30.2 million acres (12.2 million ha) of land for agricultural purposes.

RECIPE FOR EASY OATMEAL COOKIES

Oats are one of Wyoming's major crops. Follow this recipe to make some delicious no-bake oatmeal cookies.

WHAT YOU NEED:

2 cups sugar

1/2 cup milk

1/2 cup butter or margarine

1 teaspoon vanilla extract

2 1/4 cups oatmeal

5 tablespoons cocoa

Combine the sugar, milk, and butter in a pan. Have an adult help you boil this mixture on the stove. Once the mixture has boiled for around 3 minutes, add the oatmeal, the vanilla extract, and the cocoa.

Reduce the heat on the stove and stir the mixture well, making sure that the oatmeal gets cooked.

When the oatmeal is cooked, turn the stove off, and spoon the batter onto wax paper or a baking sheet.

Allow the cookies to cool and then dig in and enjoy! You can experiment with the recipe and add nuts, coconut, or raisins to the mixture after it is cooked.

A good deal of the state's farm income comes from the sale of livestock and livestock products. This is mostly cattle and calves, from the Great Plains region, and sheep. Another piece of the state's income comes from the sale of feed and cash crops. Feed crops, such as alfalfa, corn, hay, and different types of meadow grasses, are used to feed livestock. Cash crops are crops sold to food processors and to consumers in grocery stores and at other places that sell food. Cash crops grown in the Equality State include sugar beets, wheat, barley, dry beans, and potatoes.

Manufacturing

Around 3.2 percent of Wyoming's workers have manufacturing-related jobs. Most of them work in chemical plants, petroleum refineries, industrial equipment factories, food processing plants, and forest product facilities. The state's manufacturing industry plays a huge role in supplying other states with the materials they need for other industries.

Casper, with its many oil refineries, is the state's leading manufacturing center. Cheyenne, Wyoming's largest city, is well known for the manufacture of flight instruments and testing equipment. Worland and Lovell are host to refineries that process sugar beets into beet sugar. The Star Valley is the state's dairy product capital.

People who provide services to the state or its residents are part of Wyoming's service industry.

Cattle

Livestock have been a fixture on Wyoming's plains since the cattle drives of the 1870s. Most of Wyoming's agricultural income comes from the sale of beef cattle and calves.

Sugar Beets

Sugar beets are one of Wyoming's main cash crops. Sugar beets look like dark red bulbs with very large, white roots. Eastern European immigrants first brought them to the state around the end of the 1800s. Since then, farms across Wyoming have made a profit with this crop.

Coal

Coal is one of the most important minerals in Wyoming. Coal deposits lie underneath about 40 percent of Wyoming's land. Most of the mining of the mineral takes place in the state's northeastern and south-central regions. Wyoming's mines yield more than 400 million tons (363 million t) each year.

Petroleum

Wyoming is a leader in petroleum production. The state has a lot of oil in the Powder River Basin and in the part of the Overthrust Belt that is located in the state. The Overthrust Belt is a geological formation that extends from Alaska all the way to Mexico and runs through southwestern Wyoming. The belt has a large number of oil and gas reserves.

Tourism

Wyoming has been a popular tourist destination since the 1870s. In addition to scenic national parks, such as Yellowstone and Grand Teton, millions of visitors come each year to ski, hunt, and visit the state's historic towns, museums, and cultural centers. All in all, Wyoming's more than 8 million yearly visitors spend over $3 billion dollars a year.

Sheep

Sheep are an important type of livestock for Wyoming. Many ranchers herd sheep for meat but also for their wool. Every year the sheep are sheared and their coats are used to make fabrics and other material used or sold throughout the state.

Wyoming's Old West charm and amazing landscape are good for the state's tourism industry.

Service

Service industries make up the largest piece of Wyoming's GSP. People who work in service industries provide services to individuals or groups, as opposed to making a product that can be sold. Examples of workers in the service industry include teachers, salesclerks, librarians, travel agents, doctors, real estate agents, bankers, and airline pilots. Wyoming's leading service industries deal with communications, transportation, and utilities. They range from radio stations and bus companies to electric power plants.

One service industry in the state that continues to grow is tourism. Visitors come to enjoy Wyoming's outdoor attractions and to experience its culture and history. Not only is that money good for the state, but the thriving industry creates jobs for Wyomingites.

From its geography to its history to its people, Wyoming can be characterized by its variety. What is common among most Wyomingites, however, is a spirit of individualism, friendliness, dedication, and a "can-do" attitude. These are traits that make rugged Wyoming a fascinating and attractive state with a colorful past and an extremely bright future.